PRAISE FOR *MAKING SPACE FOR YOURSELF*

Erin and Bernie's collaboration brings to life ancient wisdom expressed through verse and watercolor illustrations. Each phrase and drawing captures the essential principles for loving and sharing your unique self with those around you. With the turn of every page, the reader is invited on a journey of inner reflection and self-acceptance. This lovely little book speaks the universal language of the heart, beating in unison with the longing to be fully at peace with the gift of our unique place in creation.

–Mary E. Harwood, MEd., PBC, PCC
Personal Development Coach

Making Space for Yourself is a feast for the eyes and the soul. You will be uplifted and challenged to deeply explore how you think about yourself and who you desire to become. The illustrations are glorious, will make you smile with delight and serve to move you to a deeper place inside of your spirit. The gentle questions included in the book support and guide you. It is a book to return to time and again.

–Nan Cameron, MSN, RN, LA.c

MORE PRAISE

This little book is simply lovely. The meditative imagery, empowering statements, and evocative questions weave together seamlessly, giving us, the readers, permission to pause. During an uneasy time in our shared humanity, this pause is necessary, so that we can move forward and act with intention in our greater communities. I will definitely use this book with my clients and, also, with myself!

–Hillary Rubesin, MA, LPC, REAT
Licensed Professional Counselor, Expressive Arts Therapist

Making Space for Yourself is an inspiration. The uplifting words, filled with wisdom and thoughtfulness, motivate me to be honest with my gifts and share them with others. The enlivening drawings match the words elegantly, and remind me to be creative and trust my imagination. I look forward to the creation of the whole "Drawing From the Well" series to give to friends and family.

Janice Geller, MA, LPC, LMBT

MAKING SPACE FOR YOURSELF

a guide to getting what you need

drawing from the well series

Thoughts by Bernie Kemp | Illustrations by Erin Coyle

Illustrations © 2014 and 2017 by Erin Coyle
Text ©2014 and 2017 Bernard A. Kemp

All rights reserved.

No part of this book may be reproduced or transmitted in any form or by any other means, electronic, or mechanical, including photocopying, recording, or by any information storage and retrieval system without permission in writing from the copyright holders.

ISBN: 978-0-9909655-1-0

www.drawingfromthewell.net

This book is dedicated to those who are unaware of the beauty within them.

Dear reader,

Thank you for picking up this little book. We hope that these thoughts and images spark a conversation within yourself and your community. After all, this book started from conversations between two close friends.

Even though we are friends, we have very different ways of seeing the world.

Bernie often sees things through the lens of economics--where economics is an exchange of energy. To Bernie, economics isn't all about money. However, it's about how you use your resources in the world – your energy, your time, your creativity – to create the life you want and the world you want. Bernie sees this book as a tool for meditation, contemplation and personal awareness.

Erin is an artist. She connects with and moves through the world by creatively expressing herself through art. Erin sees this book as an activating mechanism to help you learn how best to engage with the world.

Making Space for Yourself, the first of our "Drawing From the Well" series, is intended to encourage you to find your own unique way of contributing to the world. Together we hope that, by reading this book, a seed is planted —the seed of self-care. How can you and your strengths and joys give back to people or to the earth? What are you here to do? What is the contribution that only *you* can make during your limited time here on earth?

Though we are different, we have found a shared belief, which unites our work: *everything is connected to everyone and everything else.*

We share these thoughts and images with you as a helpful pathway into your own deep well of resources.

With peace and love,

Erin & Bernie

As I look back on my life, I'm reminded of what a pleasure it is to be old. Some of the self-expectations and the expectations of others dwindle away. Some friends and family have left, others have died. For this time at least, one's remaining time on Earth is limited. I encourage you to look back on your previous experiences with kindness.

WHAT WILL YOU DO WITH YOUR TIME?

HOW WILL YOU MAKE THE MOST OF YOUR TIME WHILE HERE ON MOTHER EARTH?

You are here on Earth to make a difference.
Figure out the special contribution you can make and go about it.

WHEN YOU LOOK AT THIS IMAGE WHAT DO YOU FEEL?

You are your own person, beautiful in your own right.
Own it. Stand up for it. Let it shine through.

THINK ABOUT A TIME WHEN SOMEBODY'S EXPECTATIONS MADE YOU ACT DIFFERENTLY THAN WHO YOU REALLY ARE. HOW DID THAT FEEL?

When you find your passion and pursue it, not only are you doing what you want to do, you are making those around you and the world better off. You are happy and are making a contribution. What could be better than that?

Be open and honest with yourself. Share that openness and honesty with others as you relate to them. Acknowledge your beauty, your uniqueness, and your special qualities. Honor them. By being open and honest with others you will share that beauty with them.

WHEN YOU THINK OF THE WORD BEAUTY, WHAT DOES THAT MAKE YOU THINK OF?

WHEN HAVE YOU EXPERIENCED TRUE BEAUTY?
WHEN HAVE YOU FELT TRULY BEAUTIFUL?

I'll accept you for who you are.
I hope you'll accept me for who I am.
I think you are great.

WHAT DOES BEING TRULY SEEN LOOK LIKE FOR YOU?

You never have to be somebody else. Certainly not to please someone. Just be yourself. Share that beauty—your beauty, with others—and you will find kindred spirits.

IF YOU WERE TO MAKE A COLLAGE OF YOUR CIRCLE OF KINDRED SPIRITS, WHO OR WHAT WOULD BE INCLUDED?

Your personal energy is a limited resource.
You only have so much to give. Remember,
when you are drained—when you have
committed yourself to taking care of someone or
something else without first taking care of yourself,
of your needs—you are on a course that can only
lead to problems, and perhaps to disaster.

The first step to recovering your energy and coming back into balance is to focus on yourself, on your needs. Otherwise you are expecting others to take care of you.

WHAT DOES IT FEEL LIKE TO PUT YOURSELF FIRST?

Life brings us many opportunities. With opportunity comes choice and decision.

When presented with opportunity, before you make a decision make sure you pay attention to what you are giving up.

WHAT PRIORITIES ARE MOST IMPORTANT TO YOU?

With your personal values in mind, give yourself permission to take some distance from the decision. Allow yourself the space to journal, walk, meditate, exercise, or even sleep on it. Take time to look at the opportunity from multiple angles. You'll be better informed to come to the best conclusion for you.

WHAT DOES IT LOOK LIKE TO GIVE YOURSELF PERMISSION TO PAUSE BEFORE MAKING A DECISION?

As with our time here on Mother Earth,
everything is temporary.
Enjoy this time and revel in it
while you have it. And learn from it!
It will always be part of you.
In that sense it is permanent.

WHAT IS SOMETHING YOU REALLY ENJOY?

WHAT DO YOU REVEL IN?

About the Artist

Erin Coyle is an artist and illustrator. She works in a variety of media, including watercolor, pastel, polymer, leather, and the written word. She lives in Hillsborough, NC. You can connect with Erin at www.ErinCoyle.com.

About the Author

Bernie Kemp is a nominally retired economist. He believes in the importance of continuing to make a contribution to the world. He is 89 years young and lives in Carrboro, NC. You can read more of Bernie's thoughts on his blog at www.BernieKemp.com.

We invite you to continue and contribute to the conversation about making space for yourself at

www.drawingfromthewell.net

www.ingramcontent.com/pod-product-compliance
Lightning Source LLC
Chambersburg PA
CBHW041412160426
42811CB00107B/1768